Note To Self

The LadyUp Journal

By Wanda Marie

INTRODUCTION

What a great time to be alive as a women. However, we've come so far in the fight for freedom and equality, that we have forgotten the meaning of being a Lady. This journal is a companion to the book, "*LadyUp: A Woman's Guide to Self-Defined Grace and Fearless Love.*" If you have not read the book, you may want to explore all that is said there about really rising up as a Lady, rather than continuing to be a hard working woman.

There are two ways of doing life, the King's way (through process), and the Queen's way (through grace). LadyUp is about doing life the Queen's way, with grace and ease. Rather than the effort it takes to climb a mountain, we learn how to level the mountain through pure desire.

Congratulations on being willing to fill these empty pages with your dreams, your fears, your goals, thoughts, life lessons and stories.

Whatever you do, wherever you go and whatever challenges you face in life, I have three words for you –

Be The Queen.

The Many Qualities of The Feminine

PLEASER Goddess Qualities	LEADER Queen Qualities	LADY The Goddess-Queen
Intuitive/Personal	**Intellectual/Logical**	**Wisdom/Oneness**
Spiritual Insights	**Ground Rules**	**Mystical-Knowing without Reason**
- Adaptability	- Stability	
- Spontaneous	- Structured	- Embodies and presents the Goddess or Queen energy depending on what is called for in any given moment or situation.
- In the Moment	- Mission Driven	
- Flexible	- Boundaries	
- Graceful	- Controlled	
- Service	- Leadership	- Divinity
- Inviting	- Commanding	- Space
- Honesty	- Loyalty	
- Comforter/Nurturer	- Warrior/Protector	
- Healer	- Teacher	
- Dreamer/Creator	- Builder/Destroyer	
- Playful/Inspire	- Serious/Motivate	
- Order and Beauty	- Function and Results	
- Process	- Completion	
- Open & Receptive	- Cautious/Generous	
- Authentic	- Confident	

Date:

_____

_____

_____

_____

_____

_____

_____

_____

_____

_____

_____

_____

_____

_____

_____

_____

Date:

Date:

Date:

Date:

Look in the mirror and say to yourself

"I am one with Mother Nature.
I am beautiful inside and out.

I see beauty all around me.
I create beauty all around me.

I lovingly radiate this beauty through me to
everything and everyone around me."

Date:

Date:

Date:

Date:

Date:

*Am I truly ready
to accept the responsibilities of
my purpose ~ my mission?*

Date:

Date:

Date:

Date:

Date:

"I Live an Amazing Life,

I Have Fun and Hurt No One."

Date:

_____

Date:

Date:

_____

_____

_____

_____

_____

_____

_____

_____

_____

_____

_____

_____

_____

_____

_____

_____

_____

_____

Date:

Date:

Some LadyUp Queen~isms

This or Something Better

Up Until Now

NOO (*No Other Option*)

I'm Okay, It's Okay

This is Easy…because…

I Set My Intention & Follow My Intuition

I Name It, Claim It, Own It & Done!

Date:

Date:

LadyUpNetwork.com

Date:

Date:

Date:

Grace is not something that's earned or learned. It's there for everyone—we just have to be made aware of it, connect with it, and trust the process.

Trust is a Choice

Date:

Date:

adypNetwork.com

Date:

37

Date:

Date:

Beyond the Law of Attraction is Grace.

In order to attract something, we must acknowledge that it is separate from us. This sense of separation is the greatest cause of suffering. Grace heals the separation, and all we need do is set our intention and follow our intuition.

Date:

Date:

Date:

Date:

Date:

Our intuition lies in our gut, somewhere between the spleen chakra (energy center) and the solar plexus chakra. Set your intention and follow your intuition.

THE 7 MAJOR CHAKRAS (ENERGY CENTERS)

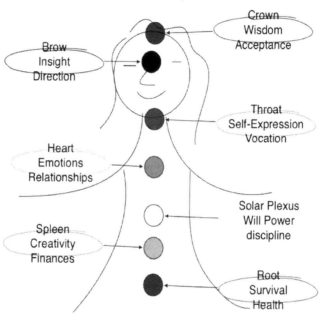

We don't let people push our buttons
and take away our power/energy.

Date:

Date:

Date:

Date:

Date:

I am divinely guided and

I trust the process of life completely.

My life is governed by grace and ease – always!

I have an amazing life!

Date:

Date:

Date:

Date:

Date:

"I love you, I see you, and I adore you."

Date:

Date:

Date:

Date:

Date:

I adore my body and I am willing to be seen.

Date:

Date:

Date:

Date:

_____

_____

_____

_____

_____

_____

_____

_____

_____

_____

_____

_____

_____

_____

_____

_____

Date:

I am beautiful, I am perfect, and I am enough.

I am healthy. I am whole and complete!

Date:

Date:

Date:

Date:

Date:

Be the Power You Possess

Date:

Date:

Date:

Date:

The clarity of your consciousness and the intensity of your feelings create your world.

Your feelings create the fuel that moves the energy (thoughts) forward into manifestation.

Mystical Manifestation =

I Name It ~ I Claim It ~ I Own It!

DONE!

This is what I am naming and claiming for my:

Finances: _____

Relationships: _____

Health: _____

Life Dream: _____

_____

Other: _____

Other: _____

Date:

Date:

Date:

Date:

Date:

All my needs are met before I know I need them.

I ALLOW THE UNIVERSE TO DO FOR ME WHAT
I CANNOT DO FOR MYSELF

Date:

Date:

Date:

Date:

Date:

Place your photo in the center.

1. Point your crystal (*or magic wand or simply use your finger*) and state your intention.
2. Begin to outline each pyramid, following the direction of the arrows as you,
3. continue stating your intention to manifest your desires.
4. Repeat as often as you want, until if feels complete – then LET GO!

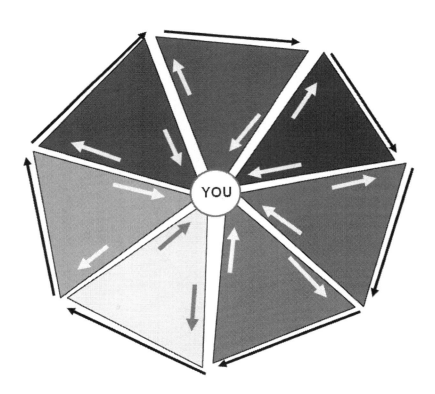

Date:

Date:

Date:

Date:

Date:

I am amazing, and I am a Queen

Check the box for each item you have mastered for living your life like a True Queen:

☐ I have learned to articulate my boundaries clearly and gracefully to others.

☐ I teach people how to treat me by standing firmly and gracefully when enforcing my boundaries.

☐ I raise my standards each year on my birthday, as a gift to myself. I allow others to love and celebrate me.

☐ I ask for what I want or need without shame or guilt, allowing others the blessings from being of service.

☐ I receive with grace, ease and humble gratitude – Always!

☐ I get that just because I can, doesn't mean I should. I always ask my higher self, "is this mine to do?"

☐ I give and/or serve others ONLY from my heart's desires to do so. I am lovingly selfish.

Date:

Date:

Date:

Date:

Date:

Practicing the Power of VAM

(Visualization, Affirmation & Meditation)

For the next 30 days, I will...

VISUALIZE MY GOAL: *(create a mental movie with you as the star. Include all 5 senses. Play the movie in your mind as you drift off to sleep each night for the next 30 days.)*

_____

_____

_____

_____

_____

_____

AFFIRM MY GOOD: *(create a positive affirmation stated in present tense to support your vison, and recite throughout each day for 30 days to counter any doubt or worry.)*

_____

_____

_____

MEDITATE FOR GUIDANCE: *(get still, relax and breathe. Ask, "what is my next step here?" Set your intention and listen to your intuition. Trust any guidance you receive and journal your thoughts each day)*

Date:

Date:

Date:

Date:

Date:

The key to a happy, healthy relationship is communication.

The key to a happy healthy relationship is having boundaries that you have the courage to, and will enforce.

The key to a happy healthy relationship is raising your standards and teaching others to honor them.

Note to Self...

How you handle the relationships in your life determines the quality of your life.

Affirmation

I am always fed, nurtured, supported, and empowered by all my relationships.

LadyUpNetwork.com

Date:

Date:

Date:

Date:

Date:

*I am a Master Giver **and** Receiver*

The Most Powerful Thing You Can Do Is "Be"

The Most Wasteful Thing You Can Do Is "Beg"

Ask, and It Is Done.

Knock, and the Door Shall Be Opened.

Date:

Date:

Date:

Date:

Date:

The Key to Life Is to Give Away the

Very Thing You Want to Attract

Be the gift you wish to receive.

Date:

Date:

Date:

Date:

Date:

When you CARE about someone,
what's important to them
becomes important to you.

When you LOVE someone,
what's important to them
becomes a priority to you.

When you are IN LOVE with someone,
they become your priority.

Date:

Date:

LadyUpNetwork.com

Date: _____

_____

_____

_____

_____

_____

_____

_____

_____

_____

_____

_____

_____

_____

_____

_____

_____

_____

133

Date:

Date:

The LadyUp Affirmation

I am a powerful and dynamic woman, filled with radiant beauty and grace. I know who I am. I am confident, wise, youthful, and poised. I am divinely guided in all that I do and say. My life is magical and everyone in my world is healthy, happy, and prosperous. I no longer need to be needed, I am whole, perfect, and complete right here and right now. My cup runneth over! And I am graceful enough to receive the overflow!

I have an amazing life!

Life is beautiful and so am I.

Date:

Date:

Date:

Date:

Date:

THE LadyUp CREED TO LIVE BY

To stand as a woman of power who commands her world with the grace of a Lady

1. We own our time and we're not afraid to charge for it.
2. We no longer struggle; we command Order in every aspect of our lives.
3. We bring and invite Beauty into our world with grace and ease.
4. We honor and promote our Passion, for self-expression as well as for profit.
5. We allow more Grace into our lives by setting our intention and trusting our intuition.
6. We honor our bodies with extreme self-care and unconditional love.
7. We are clear about who we are, always authentic, ready and willing to be seen.
8. We easily shift between the feminine qualities of innocence, seduction, and mastery.
9. We are not afraid of our power, for with it, we are wise and responsible.
10. Our Word is our wand and our sword – we can comfort the sick or slay the dragon.
11. We never withhold Love – we use it to teach, nurture, and heal.
12. We receive with grace and ease, and never negate a compliment, for we are Ladies.

Never Underestimate a LADY. She's a **Playful Goddess** *and a* **Fearless Queen.**

Date:

Date:

Date:

Date:

Date:

Date:

Date:

About the Author

Wanda Marie Lapointe is the founder of Legacy Lifestyles LLC, a North Carolina company specializing in women's empowerment and business development. She is the author of "LadyUp: A Woman's Guide to Self-Defined Grace and Fearless Love," "Living Inner Peace: A Personal Guide to Greater Happiness," and co-author, with Yolanda King, of **"Embracing Your Power in 30 Days: A Journey of Self-Discovery and Personal Freedom."** Wanda has been a Certified Master Life & Business Coach, Trainer, and Inspirational Speaker for over 25 years. She enjoys speaking to women's groups on topics such as Finding Inner Peace, Embracing Your Power, and Building Your Dreams.

A deep connection to the spiritual essence of life since early childhood caused Wanda to study various western religions and eastern philosophies, cultivating her own spiritual foundation. She spent more than 12 years as a Licensed Spiritual Practitioner/Counselor with the Agape International Spiritual Center and has traveled to the ancient land of Greece, **celebrated** Amma's (Mata Amritanandamayi) 50th birthday in Southern India, and meditated with spiritual leaders inside the Great Pyramids in Egypt.

Wanda has dedicated her life to helping women heal their lives and live their dreams. Learn more by visiting www.CoachWandaMarie.com and www.LadyUpNetwork.com.

Made in the USA
Middletown, DE
06 November 2020